The Prosecutors Fallacy, The Reliability of Fingerprint and DNA Evidence.
By
Martin Richard Thomas Allen

Introduction

Identification of a suspect is the main problem facing police forces; it is unrealistic to expect policemen to catch criminals "Red Handed". Interestingly the phrase "Red Handed" comes from the first use of forensics by Quintilian (an attorney in the Roman courts) when he showed that bloody palm prints were meant to frame a blind man of his mother's murder in approximately 1000 B.C. This is possibly the first recorded use of fingerprint technology. Amazingly fingerprints have held a fascination for many thousands of years; cavemen seemed to have painted them in many areas of the world. The first truly scientific note on the subject came in 1686 when Marcello Malpighi, a professor of anatomy at the University of Bologna, noted their characteristics. He did not however make any mention of their use as an identification tool. The first modern instance of this is by Thomas Berwick who used engravings of his fingerprints to identify his published works in the nineteenth century. The first documentation on the nature of fingerprints and their classification was written by John Evangelist Purkinji, a professor of anatomy at the University of Breslau, Czechoslovakia, but he did not realise their capacity to identify individuals. The forerunner of fingerprinting was provided with it's inspiration in the 1830's when Adolphe Quetelet, a Belgian statistician, stated that no two bodies were exactly alike. In 1856 Sir William Herschel, a British Officer working for the Indian Civil Service, used thumbprints as a replacement for signatures due to the illiteracy of the Indian population claiming benefits. In 1877 Thomas Taylor, a microscopist to the United States Department of Agriculture, suggested that the palm prints and fingerprints could be used as identification in criminal cases. This was reported in both "American Journal of Microscopy and Popular Science" and "Scientific American" but was not taken any further from this particular source. Henry Faulds, a Scottish physician working in Tokyo, went one stage further and not only published his belief that fingerprints could be used as identification evidence in the journal "Nature" but also used fingerprints to eliminate an innocent suspect and to implicate a suspect in a Tokyo burglary in 1880. In what some may consider a considerable step-back Alphonse Bertillon, a clerk in the Paris Police force, put in to place his system of anthropometry in 1883 and successfully identified a repeat offender using an alias in order to gain a more lenient sentence. Anthropometrics is the classification of a number of different measurements of parts of the body based on the theory that no two human bodies are identical. The problem with this is that clerks faced with many criminals will tend to rush or misread one or more of the multitude of the measurements, but due to the speed of the original success the system was soon implemented all over the world. In 1892 Sir Francis Galton published "Fingerprints", the first book on the nature of fingerprints and their use in crime solving. Juan Vuetich, an Argentinean police researcher, developed a fingerprint classification system in 1982 that came to be used throughout South America. Argentinia was the first country to replace anthropometry with fingerprints after Vuetich used a mother's own bloody fingerprints to implicate her with the murder of her children. In 1894 Bertillon's system which also comprised handwriting comparison, falsely implicated Alfred Dreyfus of treason. Two years later Sir Edward Richard Henry developed the classification system that would be used in Europe and North America, he also published "Classification and uses of Fingerprints". He was appointed head of Scotland Yard in 1901 and replaced anthropometrics with fingerprinting. 1903 saw the nail in the coffin of anthropometrics. At Leavenworth Federal Penitentiary, Kansas, Will West was confused with a resident convict, William West, due to the use of anthropometrics. It took until 1905 for the mistake to be realised, due to fingerprinting. The first lowest limit for fingerprint evidence was suggested in 1910 by Edmund Locard, professor of forensic medicine at the University of Lyons, France, he suggested a 12 matching point minimum. In 1977 Fuseo Matsumur, a trace evidence examiner at the Saga Prefectural Crime Laboratory of the National Police Agency of Japan, accidentally discovered the "superglue" fingerprinting technique when mounting hairs from a taxi-driver murder case. He related the information to Masato Soba, a latent print examiner; he then discovered the technique intentionally. Also in 1977 the FBI started to scan fingerprints into a database known as AFIS[1]. Sir Alec Jeffreys developed DNA profiling in 1984, he published his findings in "Nature" in 1985. In 1986 Jeffreys was called in to identify from a massive systematic DNA search the identification of the killer of two young girls in the Midlands. Coincidentally the DNA profiling led to the exoneration

---

[1] Automated Fingerprint Identification System

of a suspect. Colin Pitchfork was not found by DNA profiling, but by the bragging of the friend who took the test for him. The DNA was then found to match but it was ultimately the loose tongue of the murderer's friend which doomed the murderer. In 1986 Kerry Mullis, working for Cetus Corporation, conceived the polymerase chain reaction, a way of increasing the DNA available for testing by replication. The first commercial PCR kits were made available by Cetus Corporation in 1988.

The theory behind fingerprints is relatively simple, that no two people have identical fingerprints not even identical twins. This is because fingerprints are based on phenotype[2], not genotype[3]. The basic pattern is based on genetics, as the hand develops the hand is webbed and has pads, a throwback to our evolutionary heritage. As the foetus develops the webbing is genetically killed[4] and the webbing regresses. This process itself forms the pattern for fingerprints, but not the individual characteristics we are concerned with in fingerprinting. The pattern itself, such as loop or whorl is important in classification but that is as far as it goes. The important part is the friction ridge pattern and that is formed according to the precise temperature, pressure, motion and viscosity of the amniotic fluid that the foetus is exposed to in the womb. This explains the difference in fingerprints between identical twins. It forms the base of most criminal investigations and there is a large database of criminal fingerprints available to most police forces in the world. Taking fingerprints from a suspect is simple, it requires only for the suspect to place the tips of his fingers into ink and then place them in the correct portions of the fingerprinting card. Collection from a crime scene is only slightly more problematic. Oils, sweat etc. excreted naturally from the skin is deposited by the offender when he touches a surface and normally all that is required is a fine powder to be brushed lightly over the area to reveal the print, this print is then "lifted" by means of a cello tape type material to lift the powder from the surface. If the surface cannot be dealt with in this matter superglue could be used to develop the print in much the

---

[2] characteristics attributable to environment
[3] characteristics attributable to genetic factors
[4] Genes that enabled the webbing to grow are "turned off"

same way as a photograph, or the powder can be applied and then the print may be photographed.

DNA is more expensive and complex. The sample is identified and collected in a manner consistent with its type and sent to a laboratory. The lab then adds certain radioactive chemicals that attach to DNA sequences. These sequences are not those that code for any specific attribute but those that have been dubbed the "white noise" of DNA. Certain DNA sequences repeat themselves within the main coding sections of the DNA as a whole. These are then placed in a gel like substance and an electric current passed through the gel. The further the fragment of DNA moves the smaller it is. This is short tandem repeat DNA profiling STR for short. Profiling involves looking at certain loci or points on the DNA structure for certain patterns, radioactive chemicals that attach to these certain patterns at these certain places are then added and their retention indicates a match. A number of these chemicals are added to build up a profile. The random incident ratios for each match are then multiplied to gain the random incident ratio for the total profile.

The Current Law of Fingerprints

It has long been held by the English courts that fingerprints are unique to the individual and remain unchanging throughout life. Unlike the efforts of forensic examiners in the field of fingerprints the courts have been loath to place a minimum number of ridge characteristics as a bar to admissibility. The police and forensic examiners work to the national fingerprint guidelines which seek to place such a minimum but this does not place a bar on them presenting findings below the accepted minimum.

In R v Castleton[5], decided in 1906 identification solely on the basis of fingerprint evidence was upheld without the benefit of any numerical standard set either by the law or an examiners association. Gradually after this case a minimum of 12 ridge point characteristics was adopted, a standard which still holds in America and France to this day. The minimum merely means that above this standard, identification is proven beyond all doubt. This minimum was changed by Scotland Yard in 1924 on the basis of a paper by Alphonse Bertillon to a minimum of 16 ridge point characteristics (the prints used by Bertillon were recently found to be forgeries, therefore this minimum was adopted on a false basis).

This approach by Scotland Yard was adopted nationwide in 1953 after a meeting between the D.P.P., officials from the Home Office and representatives from various police forces in order to adopt a common approach that would bring certainty to the law of fingerprint evidence. This meeting was not designed to set a minimum for admissibility but to set the standard so high that no-one would seek to challenge the reliability of the evidence and therefore its admissibility. This brought fingerprint evidence in the eyes of the law to the pinnacle of the most reliable identification evidence that could be adduced. It was a position that was not to be challenged even by DNA. DNA must be adduced with population probability calculations but fingerprints are generally taken to be conclusive, dependant of course on the number of ridge point characteristics and the quality of the print. In the same year a conference of fingerprint experts lead to an amendment to the 16 ridge point minimum in

---

[5] 3 Cr App R 74

cases where there was already one 16 point match any further matches only needed 10 ridge point to be identified.

Over the years fingerprint examiners began to change their opinions stating that considerably less than 16 ridge points were required for a conclusive match beyond any doubt. Some even suggested 8 ridge points would provide a complete safeguard, some were so confident in their own abilities that they suggested scrapping the minimum entirely and leaving the minimum at the opinion of the examiner. This trend was followed in 1983 when a conference recognised that fingerprint examiners from around the world considered that a match with less than the English standard of that time 16 ridge points was certain. Whether this trend is a symptom of complacency on the subject of human error or the infallibility of fingerprint evidence is uncertain but the conference also decided that a numerical safeguard should also be in place and adhered to rigidly.

Recently this approach of accepting less than 16 ridge point characteristics as a point of practice has been adopted in the criminal courts. In the case of Allen[6] 12 ridge point characteristics were accepted as admissible as an exercise in discretion on the part of the judge. 12 ridge points were also held to have been properly admitted in Reid v D.P.P.[7] Mitchell J admitted evidence of 10 ridge point characteristics in R v Holt in Manchester 5th November 1996, showing further the trend towards complacency in this area of expert opinion.

R v Giles[8] in which Otton LJ presided admitted one print with 14 ridge point characteristics and one with eight, and ruled the challenge as insufficient to challenge the strength of the evidence. This showed a dilapidation of the doctrine upon which the prosecutor's fallacy was based, that fingerprint evidence was beyond challenge. At the same time the legal system enamoured with the

[6] (unreported, a decision of His Honour Judge Gordon at the Central Criminal Court, 30th June 1995)
[7] (an unreported decision, on 2nd March 1996, a Divisional Court over which Leggatt LJ presided)
[8] (unreported, Court of Appeal (Criminal Division) transcript, dated 13th February 1988)

success fingerprints enjoyed as the nail in the coffin of many criminal cases began to entertain ideas of reducing the standards required for experts to make a conclusive match.

Despite challenges the decision of the trial judge in R v Charles[9] admitted evidence of 12 ridge point characteristics. Lord Chief Justice, Lord Bingham of Cornhill said[10]:

"It was not suggested that there were differences between the two prints being compared; nor was it suggested that the similarities on which he relied did not exist. It was not, in other words, any part of the appellant's case that the prints did not match. Nor was any contradictory evidence of any kind adduced at the trial. The appellant did not call a fingerprint expert who disagreed with anything that Mr Powell said."

Lord Bingham then referred to the expert's opinion evidence that the print in question was made by the defendant.

(The expert) **"relied on the comparison between them, on the similarities and absence of dissimilarities, on his professional experience during a long career, and on his expert knowledge of the experience of other experts as reported in the literature. He concluded that the possibility of the disputed print and the control prints being made by different people could in his judgment be effectively ruled out.**

In cross-examination...he agreed that he was expressing a professional opinion and not a scientific conclusion."

This shows the degree to which fingerprint evidence is to be relied upon. As the evidence was only the opinion of the expert such factors as the experience and the standing of the expert is to be taken into account. The language used however in "effectively ruling out" the possibility of another making the print speaks again of the

---

[9] (unreported, Court of Appeal (Criminal Division) transcript of 17th December 1998)
[10] page 9E of the transcript

unassailable position fingerprint evidence has occupied for nigh on one hundred years. Can the jury also tell the difference between the professional opinion of a scientist and a scientific conclusion, surely the trap is there for a jury to take both as "science" and leave it at that? This further indicts unassailability which has lead to the presence of the so-called prosecutor's fallacy which places such evidence as fingerprints in such high regard that to even think of challenging the evidence is almost akin to blasphemy in legal circles.

1994 saw the beginning of this transition to the determination of a match being left to the expert when an ACPO report[11] recommended changing to a system with no minimum for ridge point characteristics. This was endorsed in 1996 by the Chief Constables Council. This approach was eventually adopted despite a number of challenges round the world (which will be discussed later).

R v Buckley[12] codifies the law at the moment Rose LJ has the following to say on the matter:

"That said, we turn to the legal position as it seems to us. Fingerprint evidence, like any other evidence, is admissible as a matter of law if it tends to prove the guilt of the accused. It may so tend, even if there are only a few similar ridge characteristics but it may, in such a case, have little weight. It may be excluded in the exercise of judicial discretion, if its prejudicial effect outweighs its probative value."

Rose LJ is here saying there should be some sort of direction to the jury as to the weight of the evidence. DNA which has a more digital display formula has probability possibility figures to present to the jury; perhaps such presentations should be made to the jury in fingerprint cases as well.

Rose LJ then goes to provide a number of possible tests for fingerprint evidence

---

[11] the Deputy Chief Constable of Thames Valley Police Chairing
[12] [1999] EWCA Crim 1191 (30th April, 1999)

"When the prosecution seek to rely on fingerprint evidence, it will usually be necessary to consider two questions: the first, a question of fact, is whether the control print from the accused has ridge characteristics, and if so how many, similar to those of the print on the item relied on. The second, a question of expert opinion, is whether the print on the item relied on was made by the accused. This opinion will usually be based on the number of similar ridge characteristics in the context of other findings made on comparison of the two prints. "

This is a two stage test firstly examining the control print (that made by the accused in the police station) in comparison to the print left at the scene of the crime, or on a piece of evidence, then subsequently examining the relative weight to be given to the print at the scene. This is a dangerous test unless two fingerprint experts are giving evidence. The reasons for this are that given the press coverage of fingerprints as infallible, even in such texts purposing to be written by experts in forensics the jury is likely to place more weight on fingerprint evidence than is strictly feasible. The following is an extract from such a book[13]:

"It had been known for centuries that fingerprints were unique, the ancient Chinese having used thumb impressions to seal documents, and a seventeenth century anatomist had described the ridges of fingerprints in a book"

Such books and publications based on the public's desire for detective stories with the type of plot as an Arthur Conan Doyle story require a steadfast and hyper-reliable system of identification to be presented to the jury as a fait-a-comple. This is over simplistic and liable to lead the jury into the realm of thinking they know all about fingerprints and placing over reliance on the evidence. However Rose LJ has another test also contained in Buckley:

---

[13] "Forensic Clues to Murder: Forensic Science in the art of crime detection" by Brian Marriner published by Arrow in 1991

"If there are fewer than eight similar ridge characteristics, it is highly unlikely that a judge will exercise his discretion to admit such evidence and, save in wholly exceptional circumstances, the prosecution should not seek to adduce such evidence. If there are eight or more similar ridge characteristics, a judge may or may not exercise his or her discretion in favour of admitting the evidence. How the discretion is exercised will depend on all the circumstances of the case, including in particular:

(i)   the experience and expertise of the witness;
(ii)   the number of similar ridge characteristics;
(iii)   whether there are dissimilar characteristics;
(iv)   the size of the print relied on, in that the same number of similar ridge characteristics may be more compelling in a fragment of print than in an entire print; and
(v)   the quality and clarity of the print on the item relied on, which may involve, for example, consideration of possible injury to the person who left the print, as well as factors such as smearing or contamination.

In every case where fingerprint evidence is admitted, it will generally be necessary, as in relation to all expert evidence, for the judge to warn the jury that it is evidence opinion only, that the expert's opinion is not conclusive and that it is for the jury to determine whether guilt is proved in the light of all the evidence."

This type of test presented to the jury is much more reliable as it would bring the possibility of the expert being wrong into the equation thus placing the expert witness as a human capable of human error rather than as a scientist which in the eyes of the public is an almost god-like creature in the field of science. It also brings into account that the quality of the prints and the experience of the examiner are critical in establishing such a strong indictment of the accused. In this case eight ridge point characteristics has been made a minimum for the admissibility of the evidence but this may not prove to be such a bar as is intended as the misinformation concerning fingerprints is spread to judges as well as the public. A judge is merely a more experienced lawyer and if lawyers are under the prosecutor's fallacy then surely the judiciary cannot claim to be exempt when their recruitment takes place solely from the ranks of such lawyers. In an interview[14] Michael Mansfield QC admitted that even he had fallen foul of the prosecutor's fallacy in the past and that:

"We were constantly told that to question fingerprints was like questioning two and two so we didn't."

---

[14] The Times (Fingerprints system that needs a helping hand by Jon Robins) 7 November 2000.

The Current Law of DNA

Few areas of forensic technology have captured the public imagination or interest as has DNA with new advances along the scale of the human genome project promising a physical description far more reliable than that of the typical eyewitness. However we are a long way from this particular breakthrough. Arguably the most impressive part of DNA evidence is the statistical figures produced by the forensic experts at court.

Sir Alec Jeffreys[15] quotes that the most advanced system of STR profiling using 10 different STR's (currently at use in the FSS) gives on average a 1 in 1,000,000,000 chance that two unrelated people match. This draws attention away from the fact that this, just like fingerprints is expert opinion evidence despite the different ways in which the evidence is presented. DNA being a digital system, added to the fact that the process in which it is created is understood, creates a leaning towards easier statistical analysis than the analogue system of fingerprints ever could. The USA has been both the greatest challenger and the greatest defender of this technology. One US court described DNA profiling as:

**"The single greatest advance in the "search for the truth" ......
since the advent of cross-examination"**[16]

This type of support easily misleads the public and the confidence placed in DNA evidence leads to particular legal problems. In R v Doheny[17] great care was made to point out that a random incident ratio must not be misinterpreted. The random incident ratio of 1 in 1,000,000 does not mean a one in a million chance that someone else deposited the genetic material. In a population of 25,000,000 there are theoretically 25 other people that could deposit material with the same profile. R v Doheny is the case that set the standard for both presentation and the direction of the jury in these matters. Phillips LJ addressed the problem of disclosure, how can the defence deal with a random incident ratio alone? If this was all the defence was entitled to it is of little surprise that many advocates bury their heads in the sand when it comes to the daunting task of dealing with this, the

---

[15] In Appendix 1
[16] People v Wesley, 533 NYS 2d 643, 644 (1988)
[17] [1997] 1 Cr App R 369

most challenging form of evidence for the defence. He ruled that the defence must be given sufficient details of the calculations the forensic expert is relying on to review the basis upon which they were made and if requested the databases upon which those calculations were based. This enables somewhat of an equality of arms principle in regard to this evidence with the maths being able to be scrutinised by the defence. This was particularly significant given the advantage the prosecution has over the defence in this area.

The most important development in this case was however the ruling on how the evidence was to be presented to the jury.

"the scientist should not be asked his opinion on the likelihood that it was the defendant who left the crime stain, nor when giving evidence should he use terminology which may lead the jury to believe he is expressing such an opinion."[18]

This is one of the core teachings of forensic experts:

"It is easy to make mistakes. One type of mistake is called the Prosecutor's Fallacy.
Here the evidence is misinterpreted resulting in the statement the blood is 20,000 times more likely to have come from the suspect. This might seem the same but the two statements are very different. Consider the probability that if you have a cat the probability it is an animal with four legs is 1. If you have an animal with four legs the probability it is a cat is NOT 1. It is clear when considering cats and animals with four legs, but not so obvious when considering DNA and suspects. This is a case of the transposed conditional as all probabilities are conditional of an event. In the glass case the Prosecutor's Fallacy would be to state that the glass is found at 4% then there is a 96% chance the glass can from the window."[19]

[18] page 369 and 370
[19] Forensic Science Unit, University of Strathclyde – 99.201 & 99.202
Introduction to Forensic Science

This is recognized by all as prejudicial to the defendant and to be avoided at all costs. Even judges in their summing up must be careful as to what weight they give the DNA evidence. Phillips LJ gave this sample summing up as an example as to what a trial judge should direct the jury:

"... if you accept the scientific evidence called by the Crown, this indicates that there are possibly only four or five white males in the UK from whom that semen stain could have come. The defendant is one of them. If that is the position, the decision you have to reach, on all the evidence, is whether you are sure it was the defendant who left that stain or whether it is possible that it was one of that other small group of men who share the same DNA characteristics."[20]

This hopefully will destroy the prosecutor's fallacy in its tracks leaving the DNA evidence to be evaluated on its merits. One of the greatest weaknesses of DNA is that it can never identify it merely reduces the pool of potential perpetrators to such an extent that hopefully other evidence taken into consideration with the DNA can prove beyond reasonable doubt that the accused did indeed commit the crime. This can be shown by the case of Lashley[21] in which the Court of Appeal ruled that the trial judge should have upheld the Lashley's submission of no case to answer despite the fact that the DNA profile could only have matched 7-10 men in the UK due to the absence of any collaborative evidence. In contrast with this on the same date the Court of Appeal ruled against a similar submission, where 43 other males in the UK could matched the profile, due to evidence from the Crown that the Defendant could be proven to have been at the scene 3 months after the crime.[22] Occasionally the statistics are so formidable to allow them to stand on their own as evidence of the Defendants guilt as in the case of R v Adams[23] this was indeed the case and the sole evidence was the

[20] page 370
[21] (2000) 8th February
[22] Smith (Jessie) (2000) 8th February
[23] [1996] 2 Cr App R 467 CA, R v Adams (No. 2) [1998] 1 Cr App R 377 CA
[24] (Jamaica) [2003] UKPC 9 (27 January 2003)

DNA profile adduced against the defendant. This level of reliance does put a great deal of reliance on the role of the forensic examiner. Such reliance was placed on a forensic expert in Pringle v. R[24] **"Mr Guthrie conceded that it was wrong for Dr Cruickshank to say that in her opinion the appellant was the source of the DNA in the spermatozoa in the deceased's vagina and that there was a mathematical error in her evidence about the random occurrence ratio. He accepted that the jury were misled by this evidence and that these errors went to the heart of the case against the appellant. These concessions, which were very properly made, could not reasonably have been withheld."[25]**

The forensic expert here made the two cardinal mistakes, firstly saying that the sperm came from the defendant rather than by abiding by the rules laid down in the previous case law, and secondly making a mistake in the maths of the random incident ratio. The decision in Doheny comes to mind once more due to a remark of Phillips LJ:

"The cogency of DNA evidence makes it particularly important that DNA testing is rigorously conducted so as to obviate the risk of error in the laboratory, that the method of DNA analysis and the basis of subsequent statistical calculation should – so far as possible – be transparent to the defence and that the true import of the resultant conclusion is accurately and fairly explained to the jury."[26]

The forensic examiner here managed to break most of this judgement with the possible exception of the rigorousness of the testing itself as she also used a less accurate than normal DNA test. It is only through the efforts of the defence that this was brought to light and shows the power the expert has over the jury especially in this field. However it is interesting to note that the fallacious comments were not facilitated by the prosecution, who in truth was

---

[25] paragraph 10
[26] R v Pringle (Jamaica) [2003] UKPC 9 (27 January 2003) paragraph 14 citing R v Doheny [1997] 1 Cr App R 369 pp 373-374

trying to steer his witness away from such statements but the trial judge:

"At this point the trial judge put questions to Dr Cruickshank which invited her to express her views on a matter which the prosecutor himself, so far, had been careful to avoid:
"His Lordship: Can you say where this came from?
Witness: The spermatozoa could have come from Michael Pringle.
His Lordship: When you said could have …?
Witness: In science we have 99.999 per cent certainty. So, what I would say, it is with a high degree of certainty.
His Lordship: 99.999 per cent that it came from Michael Pringle?
Witness: Yes, my Lord."
Towards the end of her cross-examination the following exchange took place between her and the judge:
"Witness: You asked me, I can't recall the question – what came to my mind – 'Why not the degree of certainty with which I state something?'
His Lordship: With which you stated that it was his semen in Kevan Davidson's vagina?
Witness: Yes.
His Lordship: And you told me it was 99.999 per cent certainty?
Witness: No. I said to you I would have to say it is with a high degree of certainty.
His Lordship: Not 99.999 …
Witness: I said 99.999. In science we say 99.99999. It goes on. But we did not address the probability in this.
His Lordship: Should I qualify this 99.999 now?
Witness: Not in the context of which we spoke. It will still stand.""[27]

The trial judge did not stop there but went on to further compound this mistake in his summing up against the advice of Phillips LJ in the Doheny case:

---

[27] paragraph 17

"When he came to this point in his summing up the judge said that the readings on the D1S80 test and on the HLADQa test on the male fraction in the vaginal swab:
"would indicate that the spermatozoa in the vaginal cavity of the deceased woman came from the accused man, Pringle."
After referring to the readings which she had obtained on the HLADQa test from the female fraction he said:
"So, it is based upon these results that she comes to the conclusion that the spermatozoa there came from Pringle, that it, that Pringle had sexual intercourse with the deceased." "[28]

This is a worst case scenario to which I will return in later chapters, but its purpose is that in contrast with Doheny, which gives the correct way to deal with DNA evidence, this is an example of the type of statements that that ruling was designed to protect against. In matters of the public and science much care must be exercised. As with the witch finder generals the almost superhuman powers of detection afforded to the scientist are above and beyond the scope of reality or common sense but in the 21st Century the scientist has almost the powers of God in the eyes of the public for he can alter the very language of life itself via genetics. Thus the courts have imposed these rules to stop the scientists getting ahead of themselves and to protect the defendant from overstatement of already overpowering odds in the eyes of his peers.

---

[28] paragraph 18

Challenges to Fingerprint Evidence

As has been noted in previous chapters fingerprint evidence has enjoyed almost one hundred years as being regarded as the most reliable type of identification evidence. Judges regard it as such; and more importantly given that most criminal trials are heard in the first instance before magistrates and juries, the public are fed this view by supposed forensic science books and the newspapers alike.

"Accurate identification of men with criminal records was and is the primary purpose of maintaining fingerprint records, though finger marks are also important clues for detectives. As statisticians have calculated that the odds against any two people having matching sets of fingerprints are actually 1 septillion (1,000,000,000,000,000,000,000,000) to one the system is very reliable."[29]

This is the type of statement that is fed to the public on a regular basis whenever fingerprints are used in a famous trial, it glosses over the fact that one septillion to one requires a set of ten fingerprints both at the crime scene and in the registration system. The odds also depend on the number of ridge point characteristics matched per print. However this is merely picking hairs with the wording of such overzealous commentaries. What is remarkable about this quote is the fact that statisticians calculated the odds. Is it not remarkable to find mathematicians dealing with calculating the odds of a biological process that even experienced doctors and anthropologists do not fully understand? We know that certain characteristics are inherited, such as the general pattern, but as to the precise conditions that cause ridge point characteristics there is no research and consequently no findings to base any such calculation on. With such ludicrous odds, statistics and untested theories in the press and our reading how can a member of the jury possibly understand the real case against the accused.

There is a wide misconception in most reading matter on this subject created for the public, that fingerprint theory has been scientifically tested. It hasn't, various evolutionists hinted at fingerprints being

---

[29] The Official Encyclopaedia of Scotland Yard (Behind the scenes at Scotland Yard) Martin Fido and Keith Skinner (2000)

different and then from nowhere without the type of widespread testing such a conclusion should have evoked it became "scientific fact".

"it's amazing to realise that one of the most well-regarded forensic techniques – fingerprinting – has never been properly put to the test. The idea that each of us has unique fingerprints has never been scientifically established – nor has the rate of errors made when matching up prints from a database with those left at crime scenes"[30]

This means that a number of cases that were decided on fingerprint evidence alone had no basis for conviction as there has never been a scientific test. Fingerprint examiners however hold themselves out to be scientists and to have a zero margin of error, this does not seem to be compatible.

Cho: **"Can't the FBI or Scotland Yard test the similarity of fingerprints by comparing prints taken from their huge archives?"**

Cole: **"The FBI did that with 50,000 prints. But they undermined the test by taking a fingerprint compared to itself as the standard for a match. They measured the similarity score that that generated. Then they ran that print against all the other 49,999 and generated similarity scores. And the similarity score for the print run against itself was higher. So they said: "Well, this proves that this print is more similar to itself than to any of the other 49,999." The problem with that is in forensics you're not comparing a print to itself. You're comparing a print to another print made from the same finger. What I think they should have done is taken one print of a finger and then another print of the same finger, not the same print, and seen what that similarity score was." [31]**

---

[30] New Scientist June 16, 2001 Editorial, Pg. 33

[31] New Scientist June 16, 2001 Opinion - interview, Pg. 4242 An identity crisis?

This is the only evidence of any testing that anyone has relied upon in the case for or against fingerprints. Other references include works by eighteenth century anthropologists or criminologists such as Darwin and Locard who may have made a hypothesis but did not have the resources to validate such a theory.

"However in all the human experience with fingerprints worldwide no two fingerprints from different digits have ever been found to match exactly. It has been argued that, since millions of sets of prints have been stored in fingerprint files as voluminous as, say, the FBI Identification Section and no exact duplication of friction skin detail has been encountered in these fingerprint repositories, individuality is clearly proved. The problem with this assertion is that it does not stand the test of reason. The millions of sets of prints were never compared against one another for possible duplication of friction ridge patterns. Filing and retrieving prints from such a massive file only results in an examination of a comparatively small number of sets of prints: those with a matching, or approximately matching, classification formula."[32]

This means that with a large selection of fingerprints not all of them are checked against each other as a large number of fingerprints are discounted by the filing system as more than one print comes in at once.

Cho: **"In 1993, the US Supreme Court said that scientific evidence had to be testable, subject to scrutiny by other scientists, accompanied by quantitative estimates of uncertainty, and generally accepted by the scientific community. Does fingerprinting meet these standards?"**

Cole: **"I don't think it meets any of them. I don't think fingerprint examiners have tested their claim – which is that they can reliably match a latent print to one and only one finger**

Interview of Simon Cole by Adrian Cho
[32] Is Fingerprint Identification a "Science"? By Andre Moenssens (www.forensic-evidence.com)

to the exclusion of all others in the world. They continually refuse to calculate an error rate for fingerprinting; believing that having a zero error rate will make them more scientific, even though among hard scientists a zero error rate would be cause for suspicion. Peer review and general acceptance are somewhat fuzzier criteria. The question is whether fingerprint examiners have created such a closed community that peer review is meaningless. There are ways in which astrology can meet the peer review requirement."[33]

Can we really say that jumping to such a conclusion with hardly any evidence is scientific? For this is how the jury sees the forensic expert, as a scientist and a reliable one at that. As has already been noted experienced lawyers cringe in the face of such opposition. It has been noted even in the United States of America where there have been numerous challenges to forensic evidence.

"Your client looks at you across your desk, his eyes glistening with as much sincerity as you've ever seen, and says plaintively, almost silently, "I know what the lab report says, but I swear, It's not my _____." (Fill in the blank with any one or more of the following as appropriate): blood, gun, fingerprints, DNA, tool mark, semen, hair, fibre, handwriting, shoe impression, or toothmark.
The guy seems totally believable, but you too have read the lab report and so you know, I mean like, really know, it is indeed his blood, or hair, or whatever ... says so right in the crime lab report's section on "Results". It's enough to make you think to yourself; "This guy would make a great witness. Even I can't tell he's lying".[34]

A clear case of the prosecutor's fallacy, it's in the report so it must be true. A version of the scenario described above happened in Scotland in the year 2000. A policewoman called Shirley McKie was

[33] New Scientist June 16, 2001 Opinion - interview, Pg. 4242 An identity crisis? Interview of Simon Cole by Adrian Cho
[34] A Beginner's Primer on the Investigation of Forensic Evidence By Kim Kruglick (www.scientific.org)

charged with perjury for saying she had never been at the crime scene. Her fingerprints had supposedly been found at the crime scene and she was charged despite having eyewitness testimony of over two hundred witnesses saying she had never been anywhere near the scene. A fingerprint expert from the USA and one from Scotland Yard were called in by the defence as expert witnesses and both were astounded by the supposed "match."[35]

"Now, after all these years, fingerprint evidence and it's granddaughter, DNA, are coming under renewed scrutiny. There is an article by Michael Specter 'Do Fingerprints Lie?' in The New Yorker (27 May). It centres on the Scottish case of policewoman Shirley McKie whose print was apparently found in a room where the murder took place. She said she had not been there and was prosecuted for perjury. Fortunately, a senior New Scotland Yard scientist was convinced it was not her print. 'It wasn't even a close call', he said, and she was vindicated."[36]

The quality of the prints were not good and it is astounding that a match could even be found, on one a large part of the print containing the delta (one of the main identification and classification points) is not even present yet the missing area is used as identification (in the picture on the left points 7, 8 and 10 all point to the area that is obliterated and in the picture on the right points 6, 7, 8 and 9 also do this).

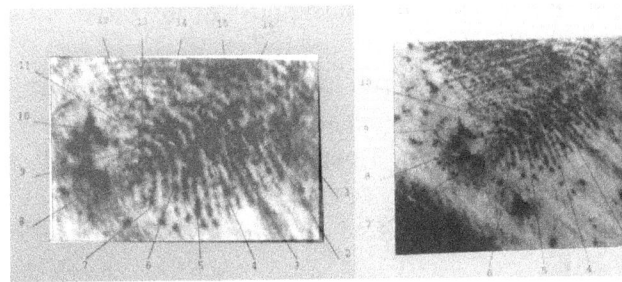

Above are the actual crime scene fingerprints and the supposed ridge similarities. Below are the file versions that were claimed to match

---

[35] The Times 7 November 2000 – Fingerprints system that needs a helping hand by Jon Robbins
[36] Pointing the finger By James Morton Law Gazette 2000

the crime scene prints but are in reality Shirley McKie's prints. Each fingerprint on the left side of the page is supposed to match as with the prints on the right.[37]

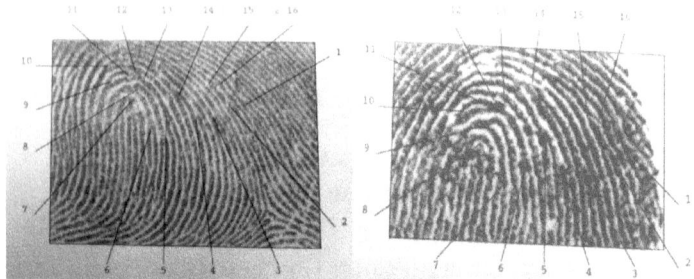

This brings us to the bread and butter of challenges to forensic evidence, the chance of a mistake. Shirley McKie was blatantly the victim of a mistake. Her fingerprints did not match so there must have been a mistake. A recent secret study in America yielded some surprising results in relation to competency in fingerprint examiners.

Cho: **"What's the evidence on the reliability of those examiners?"**

Cole: **"A new proficiency test, designed in conjunction with the International Association for Identification, was conducted by an independent testing service starting in 1995. And that first test yielded this horrible error rate of 22 per cent for false positives – matching a print to the wrong print. In the law enforcement context that could mean a false conviction. That got everyone upset in the fingerprint community. Subsequent tests revealed error rates ranging from 3 per cent to 15 per cent. You can always deconstruct proficiency tests and complain that they're not a real representation of what's going on. But they're the best guess we have."[38]**

---

[37] Copies of the prints found on http://onin.com/fp/mckievindication.html (a website run by Shirley McKie's father, which has now been updated to reflect the apology given by the Scottish investigating authority).
[38] New Scientist June 16, 2001 Opinion - interview, Pg. 4242 An identity crisis? Interview of Simon Cole by Adrian Cho

This shows an error rate of almost a quarter of the time and over a fifth. That means one in five fingerprint matches could be wrong. It must certainly be noted at this point that while the science may be reliable it is only as reliable as those performing the test.

"In January of this year, a US District Court judge limited the use of fingerprint evidence in a Philadelphia murder case. He noted the 'alarmingly high' error rates on periodic proficiency exams."[39]

With such a high margin of error and untrained individuals realizing that this type of thing is happening it shows that a large number of individuals are below the standard of a "zero" error rate that fingerprint experts are generally awarded by judges and jury.

These are the types of challenges that most lawyers will want to come up with. Perhaps the examiner made a mistake or the odds were wrong and that one in a septillion person came up. It's no-one's fault, just one of those things or simple carelessness, no harm was meant. However there is still one area of challenge left that has not been widely reported. The very aura of invincibility of fingerprints gives them enormous power and it was only a matter of time before that was taken advantage of. Despite police protestations that:

"The likelihood of fraudulent production of prints is negligible, since as in all cases where "framing" by police technicians is postulated, the number of people necessarily involved in any such conspiracy would make it completely impracticable."[40]

Well however unlikely and impracticable this is precisely what has happened in America. Fingerprints were forged and used in courts of law, and no-one even challenged them.

---

[39] Pointing the finger By James Morton Law Gazette 2000
[40] The Official Encyclopaedia of Scotland Yard (Behind the scenes at Scotland Yard) Martin Fido and Keith Skinner (2000)

"One good example of this is the scandal surrounding the New York State Police, when it turned out that state troopers had been fabricating extremely crude, transparently fake fingerprint evidence and using it to secure numerous murder convictions. In no case did the defense lawyers question the evidence or hire experts to look at it."[41]

When a weapon of this power goes off the rails the consequences are disastrous. We need to question supposed miracles of modern science that can prove guilt or identity because it is not just the test itself but the motives and care of the people performing the test that must be examined. The checks are there to be used, not to allow people to assume everyone will do a 100% error free, ethical job 100% of the time. If anything is a fallacy then thinking in that way is.

[41] New Scientist June 16, 2001 Opinion - interview, Pg. 4242 An identity crisis? Interview of Simon Cole by Adrian Cho

Challenges to DNA Evidence

Many high profile rape and murder cases hinge on the production by the prosecution of DNA evidence but the reliance placed upon DNA has now surpassed that enjoyed by fingerprints even though it has only been used for a fraction of the time that fingerprints have. While both fingerprints and DNA are regarded as "science" DNA also enjoys a reputation as "digital". While fingerprints are examined by humans, the jurors are convinced that the dark lines they see are beyond doubt matches. This is due to the nature of DNA itself, the structure of DNA is digital (i.e. that the gene in question is an A, C, G or T), there are only four possible outcomes. However, how digital are the readouts the "scientists" analyse?

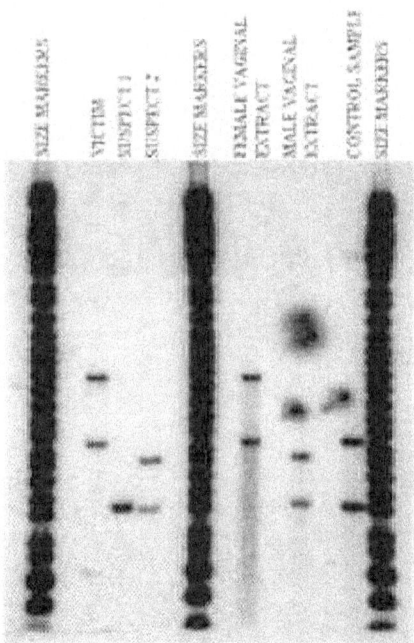

This autoradiogram is taken from a rape case in America[42], and it is evident that the evidence from the male vaginal extract is very blurry near the top and exactly what inferences to be made are hardly easy to read for a lay person. This undermines our view that DNA does not require any interpretation in checking for a match, a fact that seems to be lost to most people who accept DNA readily as proof of guilt without even checking the facts of the matter. A Florida study

---

[42] People v Marshall (Los Angeles County Superior Court, No BA 069796, 1996)

found that 83% of judges could not distinguish valid from flawed scientific evidence.[43] How is the jury to make a decision on the validity of the evidence presented to it if the judge who presumably has sat through cases like this before cannot even perform the same task and offer them guidance on how to make the descision?

"I give my lectures on DNA to Ph.D.'s in other fields, and it's hard for them to absorb it all. The average juror would need a two-week course to be able to judge any comment on DNA evidence."[44]

The prospect of a two week course just to begin a complex trial would not only put off jurors but positively bias them against the defence team that took them out of their lives for such tedium. This coupled with their tendency to think that DNA is infallible means that the defendant is at a considerable disadvantage when it comes to trying to establish his innocence.

"Juries think science is so absolute that DNA evidence is without question."[45]

Many commentators and lawyers have noticed this trend from the outset of DNA evidence. This may come from the hope placed on DNA research to cure cancer, MS and other such genetically related disorders. It also stems from the statistics adduced to show the reliability of the evidence by the prosecution experts.

The statistics adduced by such experts are just that, statistics evidencing probability, the difference between textbook probability theory and events in reality are hardly ever explained to juries.

---

[43] Reported at the Second Annual National Conference on Science and the Law at the National Institute of Justice in June 2002
[44] Conrad Gillam, professor of genetics and development at Columbia University USA in "DNA as a forensic instrument" by Mark Fishetti on the Columbia University website
[45] Charles Leonard, partner in Tremper, Bechert & Leonard in Fort Wayne, Indiana and court appointed defender in Indiana v Hopkins, the third case involving DNA evidence in the USA. Reported in "DNA as a forensic instrument" by Mark Fishetti on the Columbia University website

Theoretically it is possible to spin a coin and it will come down heads every time, which in the eyes of the jury is impossible as they know the probability of a coin coming down as heads once is 50% and thus the coin should come down heads 5 times and tails another 5 times. But what is not presented to the jury is the probability of a false match based on the size of the database used. According to Sir Alec Jeffreys the odds of such an occurrence in the UK based on the size of the UK police database is 1 in 500[46]. That means that one in five hundred cases could be falsely matched. This is without any allegation of negligence or misinterpretation on the part of the forensic scientist. Other attempts to equal out this large differential between the presentation of evidence have been attempted. The court of Appeal has had to rule on the application of "Bayes theorem" on a number of occasions. In simple terms "Bayes theorem" is a way of presenting more mundane evidence in a statistical manner so that it can be presented in the same way as DNA evidence. However the drawbacks of this are evident:

"(Bayes theorem) is not appropriate for use in jury trials, or as a means to assist the jury in their task …(T)he theorem's methodology requires … that items of evidence be assessed separately according to their bearing on the accused's guilt, before being combined in the overall formula. That is far too rigid an approach to evidence of the type that a jury characteristically has to asses…"[47]

This was a failed attempt by the defence to put all evidence on an equal basis but the application of such complex mathematical formulae would simply put the jury off the defence's arguments.

The danger of DNA is not in all cases but where it is the only evidence relied upon or the collaborative evidence is so flawed as to have almost no bearing on the case. As in a case reported in the Daily News on February 11th 2000 where a man was arrested despite alibi evidence to the contrary for burglary. This was due to a six loci DNA test which the police claimed identified him as the perpetrator.

---

[46] Letter to author
[47] Adams [1996] 2 Cr App R 467 decision by Rose LJ

This may seem like an open and shut case until the rest of the facts are revealed. The man lived 200 miles away from the crime scene, was babysitting his baby daughter at home and suffered from Parkinson's disease in an advanced state and as a result could not drive or even tie his own shoelaces or dress himself. The police dismissed these arguments as due to the DNA results "it had to be him" the odds of another match were apparently one in thirty-seven million. The suspect was released after months in jail when his solicitor demanded a retest on 10 loci. This test showed that on the new four loci his DNA did not match. This shows the strength of faith in DNA over common sense and overriding defence evidence. There was no way that the suspect could have committed the crime in question. The man in question still awaits an apology from the police force in question.

We come now to the possibility of examiner bias when examining the DNA autoradiogram. The possibility of error here is thought to be minimal as we have all seen the neat crisp images of such results where it is clear as to the bands but as seen in the autoradiogram above this is not always the case. I return to People v Marshall[48] as evidence of this. There were two autoradiograms taken in this case. Two black males were charged with abducting and raping a woman. The woman could not identify her assailants and so DNA was the only way of achieving this.

"According to the laboratory report, "DNA banding patterns obtained from the male fraction of the vaginal aspirate demonstrate DNA from two individuals consistent with the patterns obtained from [the two suspects]." The DNA patterns of Suspect 1 (Marshall) "occur with a frequency of one in 641,100,000 in the North American Black population" and the patterns for Suspect 2 "occur with a frequency of one in 636,500,000 in the North American Black population." The laboratory report gives no indication of any uncertainty about the "match" between the suspects and the vaginal sample, so it would appear that the DNA test provides damning evidence against both suspects."[49]

---

[48] (Los Angeles County Superior Court, No BA 069796, 1996)

There are two autoradiograms to consider in this case. These are shown below and are the autoradiograms from the case itself. Figure 1 has been enhanced to show the pen marks made by the forensic examiner by marking in black pixels in "Microsoft Paint" but no other alterations were made.

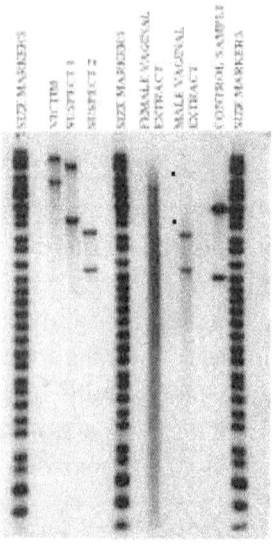

Figure 1

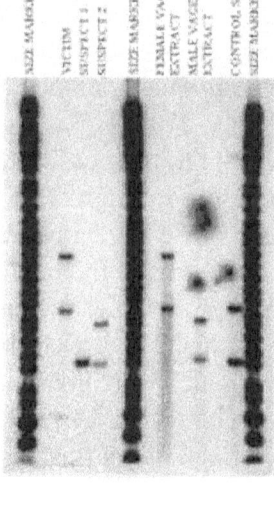

Figure 2

In figure 1**"The key comparison is between the suspects' patterns** [lanes 3 and 4 from the left] **and the pattern in the male vaginal extract** [lane 7 from the left or lane 3 from the right]. **Two bands corresponding to those of Suspect 2 are clearly visible, indicating that he is a possible source of this DNA. Whether bands corresponding to those of Suspect 1 are also present is less clear. The two dots on the left side of this lane are felt tip pen marks made by the forensic analyst to indicate where he thought he saw bands.**[50] **However, other experts were sceptical about whether**

---

[49] Examiner Bias in Forensic RFLP Analysis by William C. Thompson published in Scientific Testimony An Online Journal

the presence of bands could be reliably determined. And one expert thought the upper-most "band" in the male vaginal lane, if present, did not align closely enough with the upper band of Suspect 1 to be called a match."[51]

In figure 2 **"However, it is impossible to tell from this autorad whether a pattern corresponding to that of Suspect 1 appears in the vaginal extract because the only band matching his could be accounted for by the DNA of Suspect 2. Additionally, the upper portion of the male vaginal extract lane contains dark blotches, caused by technical problems in the assay that may obscure bands of the second rapist."**

This clearly shows the subjective nature of the borderline cases of identification by DNA evidence. However this case has yet more to offer in the way of subjectivity as William C. Thompson continues he was the co-counsel for Suspect 1 and he suspected examiner bias in the case. So he asked for the tests to be re-run in his presence as the examiner maintained that the computer running the tests detected the bands and the process was completely objective.

"During this re-scoring, the claim that the process was objective evaporated. In order to detect bands in the male vaginal extract lane that corresponded to those of Suspect 1, the analyst had to increase the sensitivity band of the computer to the point that it detected many additional "bands" that matched neither suspect. The analyst then performed a "manual override" of the computer's scorings, instructing the computer to "delete" (i.e., ignore) all of the bands that matched neither suspect. An image of the autorad appeared on a computer screen, with green lines indicating places where the computer had detected a "band". The analyst was able to delete any bands that were not deemed to be "true" bands through a simple point and click operation

---

[50] These pen marks were enhanced as stated above to make them clearer on the printout of this document. The rest of the image has remained unaltered.
[51] Examiner Bias in Forensic RFLP Analysis by William C. Thompson published in Scientific Testimony An Online Journal

with a computer mouse. The software program also allows an analyst to re-position the "bands" using the mouse.

When asked to state the basis for deleting some bands while leaving others, the analyst responded that he could "tell by looking" that the undeleted bands (which happened to match my client) were true bands, while the others were not. A number of the deleted bands had higher optical densities than the bands scored as matching my client. So much for objectivity."[52]

This is a disturbing case, the evidence presented as a) objective and b) reliable was not objective due to the human intervention of the analyst and it's reliability must be seriously doubted due to the tampering involved in the "reliable" process. Even with the tampering the bands in figure 1 are so faint as to be virtually invisible and the blotchiness of figure 2 makes any comparison highly suspect and dangerous. This type of behaviour may be attributed to an attempt to help rather than abuse of power or negligence.

"I heard one forensic analyst defend the scoring of an ambiguous band (a judgement that incriminated a defendant in a rape case) by saying "I must be right, they found the victim's purse in [the defendant's] apartment."[53]

Examiner objectivity must be maintained at all costs in such cases; especially those involving rape, murder and paedophilia for such crimes are so reviled as to attract an aura of guilt to anyone who is accused and with forensic examiners working with such preconceived ideas the accused will be found guilty by virtue of reconfigured evidence or evidence that is highly dubious if the defence lawyer is cowed by the reputation of the process itself. If such procedures are not in place we return to the dark days of justice, those of the Witchfinder Generals, Salem Witch Trials and

---

[52] Examiner Bias in Forensic RFLP Analysis by William C. Thompson published in Scientific Testimony An Online Journal
[53] Examiner Bias in Forensic RFLP Analysis by William C. Thompson published in Scientific Testimony An Online Journal

McCathyist Anti-Communism where guilt is assumed and the evidence cannot be challenged, the accuser has ultimate power and justice takes a backseat to the prejudices of the scientists. This obviously is a worst-case scenario; most forensic examiners take their jobs seriously and endeavour to produce fair results as this is the best way to secure a conviction of the true criminal whether he is currently on trial or not. However the potential is there if DNA remains as it is, in reality though not in law, a reversal of the burden of proof.

Corporations and DNA Evidence

So far we have looked at challenges to and for the evidence itself with reference to both DNA and fingerprint evidence. What has not been examined is the effect of the monetary aspect of the businesses that deal with the production of the test kits. While the testing process is carried out in England by the Forensic Science Service (a government body independent of the police) the tests are manufactured by a small range of companies. It is these companies who are competing in an increasingly competitive market. Also the Forensic Science Service hires private laboratories when their caseload is so high as to cause significant delays.

"But money too can play a role in an effective cross-examination. A two minute search of the internet disclosed that during a recent capital murder case a major, nationally known lab hired by the DA settled a fraud suit brought by the US Government for $187 million. You can predict the argument to the jury … If a lab engages in wholesale fraudulent practices, how can we trust their test results? It's a falsus in uno, falsus in omnibus kinda argument."[54]

These companies produce the initial statistics as to how reliable their own product is i.e. the random incidence ratio that often reaches the billions and is presented to the jury. There are only a few manufacturers of these kits in the US and they have recently started expanding into the UK. Cellmark has recently been merged with a US company, bringing the cutthroat US market to British Biotech.

"The financial interest of prosecution experts is a primo area for cross. This results from the fact that there are only a few manufacturers of the DNA "kits" used throughout the country and the competition is fierce. The same folks that produce kits own several of the labs that perform forensic DNA tests. Any assault on the scientific integrity of the testing, or the kit, aims right at the scientists Achilles heel of corporate profits. By the way, check out the prosecution experts. These folks often have

---

[54] A Beginner's Primer on the Investigation of Forensic Evidence By Kim Kruglick (www.scientific.org)

stock or an ownership interest in the lab. A good area for crossing on bias and interest."[55]

Any scientist whether motivated for a just decision or not has motives for the success of his testing, he requires work just like everyone else. These scientists are rewarded as much as lawyers for their appearances in court and if they show weakness on the stand and subsequently loose the case on the basis of the forensic testing they will not be chosen by the lab to appear in court again simply because it will reflect badly on the kit that is produced and the police / Forensic Science Service / private laboratories will start to use someone else's kit as it seems more reliable.

"Whether or not current guidelines require such publication, the court is troubled by the lack of publication of primer sequences. Proprietary information or not, the lack of transparency is disturbing."[56]

This approach completely inhibits the scientific community validating whether the test itself even works let alone the random incident ratio statistics published by the company that developed it. Justice must be seen to have been done, that means that the defence must have access to the data that is convicting the accused, especially in such circumstances as when DNA is adduced.

"As the court has noted twice above, the failure of the manufacturers of DNA testing systems to disclose the primer sequences they have created to permit amplification of DNA is problematic from the perspective of scientific knowledge and, consequently, validation. It is more than problematic; it is anti-scientific in that it inhibits the ability of scientists in the field (including defence experts) to test the manufacturer's claims. Although the court understands that the manufacturers believe that they need to maintain as confidential what they consider to

---

[55] A Beginner's Primer on the Investigation of Forensic Evidence By Kim Kruglick (www.scientific.org)

[56] State of Vermont v Michael Penning Filed at Grand Isle Courts on April 6th 2000

be proprietary information, in the case of new technology, it delays acceptance by the courts. In view of the mandate of Streich – particularly the first and second factors – the results of the Profiler Plus tests cannot be admitted."[57]

Thus we can see the manufacturers are enthusiastic about piping the competition to the post and developing newer and newer tests that test more and more sequences and make defending a DNA case yet more and more problematic, yet they seem to omit proper testing in their rush to get a new kit on the market.

"it also highlights the fact that the system at issue here is still relatively new and thus the evidence presented in support of that system is still being developed. Therefore the court finds that, at this point in time, the multiplex technique employed by the Profiler Plus and Cofiler kits has not been generally accepted in the scientific community. Therefore these tests are not admissible against Mr Shreck."[58]

Then we come to the problem of the examiners themselves, many of which do their jobs in the interests of justice, but where there is money to be made it is the sad fate of the human race to find someone willing to take advantage of that position. Thankfully there has been no evidence of anyone having used their position as a forensic scientist to frame anyone, but that does not of course mean it is not possible, you do certainly get experts who should not be allowed to act as such due to incompetence or bias, see, for example, R v Stubbs[59] and Huxley v Elvicta Wood Engineering Ltd.[60]

"Although Dr. Budowle testified that the method has been generally accepted and is reliable despite the lack of validation per TWGDAM, under the circumstances, the Court does not feel

---

[57] State of Vermont v Michael Penning Filed at Grand Isle Courts on April 6th 2000

[58] The People of the State of Colorado v Michael Eugene Shreck Case Number 98CR2475; Division 4

[59] [2002] EWCA Crim 2254

[60] LTL 19/4/2000

it can rule on this testimony alone. The Court does not doubt Dr. Budowle's credentials. They are impressive, impeccable and inspiring. However, Dr. Budowle is not entirely disinterested. He was instrumental, in the development and promotion of these kits. One of his primary goals from the beginning was uniformity in testing and adoption of the system by the laboratories which would be providing data to the national CODIS databank. Consequently, he has a vested interest in seeing the system succeed. He has expended considerable time, energy and funds to this end and has much to lose if these results are inadmissible in court. Although the Court does not doubt his professional expertise, nor his view that the kits are reliable, under these circumstances, the Court can not rest its decision on his word alone."[61]

Even though scientists may not let their interests interfere with their work justice must be seen to be done and experts should be a stage removed from their interests with their professional opinions.

The companies producing these kits seem to have lost sight of their importance. These kits are to provide justice and to catch the correct criminals for the correct crimes. Their aim is not to provide as many convictions as possible and thus fill the coffers. We must be careful in administering justice for all too often it can go wrong. As the old axiom goes, it is better by far to let one hundred criminals go free than to imprison one innocent man. We must not let the sight of profits blind us to interests of justice and ultimately to the needs of humanity.

---

[61] The People of the State of Colorado v Michael Eugene Shreck Case Number 98CR2475; Division 4

Fingerprints and DNA in the Future

In the future scientists hope to be able to codify the entire human genome as a method of eradicating such deficiencies as Down syndrome, Bi-polar Disorder and other genetic disorders. Such codification will have the effect of producing a physical description of anyone from their DNA thus helping the police track down the perpetrator so they can take his DNA in the first place. This gap between having the criminal's DNA and finding someone to test is the gap that the police next need to fill for it is all very well to say we have the suspects DNA, but it could be anyone! To fill this gap there are proposals in America to have national ID cards that have retina scans or DNA information on them as proof of identity. Is DNA so reliable that it could support such a system? True, it's digital nature and the complexity of the code makes it ideal for identification purposes, but is our testing up to that ideal standard? A national database would reduce the risks of a false match from the 1/500 previously mentioned.[62] This is because the size of the database would be increase from the current size of 2,000,000[63] to the size of the population of Britain. It would also provide an opportunity to gain empirically true results as to he repetition of the various genes, loci etc. which are currently estimated by statisticians on the basis of small samples of DNA and population data based on a small sample group. The new nationwide DNA database could then be searched for these statistics giving a large sample group and a true representation for nationwide representation rather than speculation as exists now. This however relies on testing of 100% accuracy and an ability to narrow down the odds of a match to a number greater than that of the total population of the country in question. This presumption would only really work if the borders of Britain were closed but given the many influxes of foreign DNA over the course of history really means that such a system could only work with odds that individualise one person from the rest of the world's population given the fluidity of today's world population.

Over the past 2,000 years DNA has come into the mainstream of the British gene pool from the Roman Empire, which included most of Europe, part of the African continent and parts of Asia. The Saxon

---

[62] Appendix 1
[63] Appendix 1

invasions brought DNA from the Germanic peoples of Europe. Viking settlements brought Scandinavian DNA to most of the East coast and as far inland as the Midlands. The French invasion in 1066 brought yet more French DNA. Then we must factor in the impact of the British Empire from the 15th Century onwards. Then the influx of Jamaican, Indian, Pakistani and other Asian communities into Britain in the 1950's onwards all have now started to dilute the gene pool even more. Britain has one of the most diverse gene pools in the world due to its place in the global community over this time period. According to Darwinian Theory the most successful genes will survive in such circumstances and the least successful will die out leading to a limited number of variations in the populous (ruling out the possibility of mutation which will be dealt with later). This diversity allows non-British persons to appear British in their DNA patterns and increase the risk of a false match when they pass through our borders. The fluidity of global population as evidenced by the treaties of Europe protecting the free movement of workers means that population counts in one country to determine the reoccurrence ratio of DNA strands are ultimately flawed. This of course is in the face of international crime of which there is relatively little but it still occurs and with border breakdowns along the lines of the European Community is set to rise especially in relation to random crime in which DNA is usually instrumental in solving.

New medical science can also frustrate DNA fingerprinting; there are already a number of ways which a resourceful criminal can avoid a DNA match, if he can find an unscrupulous enough doctor.

Mutation is a well known tool of evolution, it produces new DNA combinations in ways that sexual reproduction would take a much longer time to combine, if at all. In most cases this is harmless and produces no real change as it affects the "white noise" section of the DNA. Coincidentally this is also the area tested in DNA fingerprinting. However many DNA mutations are destroyed by the immune system before they can spread or they result in Cancer. But a beneficial mutation, which is unlikely, could spread though the body changing the DNA of the individual enough to frustrate a DNA match.

Gene therapy, currently in development, uses a retrovirus to insert DNA into the lining of the lungs using a inhalation spray. This is hoped will cure genetic disorders by removing the gene that causes the problem and replacing it with a "normal" gene from another person. Used on a criminal, in theory, the DNA could be so reformatted as to completely avoid a DNA match.

Identical twins are also another problem area for DNA, they have identical DNA coding and also appearance and so are very hard to differentiate without any other evidence. The Railiens have now added to the future uncertainty surrounding identical genetic structures by claiming that they have cloned two human beings. The impact of this on DNA evidence will not be felt for many years, if at all, due to the length of time needed for the clones to reach adulthood. Also legislation in many developed countries now also outlaws the cloning of human beings. However the question still remains what will stop someone in twenty years from denying DNA evidence points to them by reason that they are one of the Railien Clones? Given the secrecy of the cult itself could anyone use this defence of would a real clone be convicted on the basis that no real proof exists for the existence of human clones (a view that was propagated in many forms of media by scientists and governments alike when the Railiens made their controversial announcement). It is known that other organisms have been cloned so it is theoretically possible that human clones have been created. Maybe we shall never know the true impact of this, as the courts will need a test case in order to make a ruling and the likelihood of this happening is extremely remote.

All of these possible ways around DNA are borderline cases, the odds of any of these situations occurring are very limited indeed but the important point is that they are possible and may occur at any time in the future thus rendering DNA evidence even with the elusive 100% reliability inconsequential as far as that case is concerned, thus undermining the stability of the process itself in the courtroom even with the proper checks imposed.

Fingerprints conversely have shown themselves to be remarkably resistant to alteration. The only way to alter your fingerprints is to gain a scar on the finger pad itself. Attempts to alter fingerprints have included a regular burning off of the print using acid and then letting the prints grow back in the vain hope that they would be different when they returned. They were still the same. One man had his fingerprints removed and a skin graft from his palm taken to replace the skin on his fingers. Unfortunately for him he had left a palm print at the scene of the crime and this was used to convict him. In terms of alteration fingerprints are the most reliable way of identifying a suspect, if all the above ways of altering identification are available to a criminal. Interestingly in the film "Diamonds are Forever" James Bond manages to pass a fingerprint test using fake prints on a cling film type surface adhered to his fingertips. This may be a way of circumventing the reliability of fingerprint tests in the future by criminals but at the moment it is in the realm of science fiction and not currently possible. Currently criminals in America are using a low-tech variation on this; they use the skin from the tips of the fingers from corpses to leave fake fingerprints at the crime scene in order to put the police on the wrong track.

The advances in identification are always followed shortly afterwards by ways around it. Eyewitness identification can be avoided by plastic surgery, retina scans can theoretically be avoided using specially designed contact lenses (as per Mission Impossible, starring Tom Cruise) and more ways will become available to circumvent DNA and fingerprint identification as our understanding of these phenomena becomes more advanced. However sacrosanct a form of ID is the criminal and scientific mind will devise ways round it giving each form an inbuilt shelf life which will be abused by the criminal element.

Conclusion

Mankind in this Century seems to be moving away from a belief in God to a belief in a much more manmade ideal, that of science. We all look back in scorn at those who believed the earth was flat and that the sun revolved around it. We elevate Copernicus and Leornardo Da Vinci to ideals, an almost deity type reverence. Those who challenge accepted "scientific" accepted norms are looked upon as troglodytes and ridiculed. We have elevated scientists to a status akin in our society to that of God. In fact DNA has been referred to as the language of God[64], a divine code that defines each and every one of us. We ignore the warnings from those we refer to as scaremongers who see the scarier side of this development. The film "Gattica" showed widespread discrimination on the genetic level due to the ability in the film of humans to manipulate the human genome an engineer the perfect human. This we say would never happen, despite witnessing the Second World War and the Holocaust in which the same thing happened albeit on a more crude level. The film "Minority Report" showed the same type of thing in respect to a "Criminal Gene" something scientists claim to be near finding. This is a frankly scary idea, given the digital nature of DNA, one either has the gene or one does not. Thankfully this type of testing will not occur in my lifetime. What is happening however is no less frightening, the image of an infallible proof of guilt undermines the very issue of justice. We find ourselves returning again and again to the type of trial found in the darkest points in history. In England we had the Witch-finder Generals, in Spain the Spanish Inquisition, America had both the Salem Witch trials and the McCarthy Communist outings, while Russia had the show trials. A "scaremonger" of the 50's witnessing the McCarthy era joined these images in a classic play which contained a quote that refers to the loss of justice for an impossible burden of guilt. The play was "The Crucible" by Arthur Miller, when John Proctor is finally accused of witchcraft despite revealing the malice that caused the entire ordeal, to his own detriment, he says the following:

"I think, you are pulling down Heaven and raising a whore!"

---

[64] Watson and Crick in "DNA" broadcast by Channel 4 in December 2002/ January 2003

This is a comment on justice that can be applied to the current situation on DNA and fingerprints. Justice is being undermined and replaced with such an impossible test of innocence that one must now prove innocence not rely on being proven guilty.

We rely on tests that themselves have not been tested, we grant status of infallibility to those that are human and thus must by definition make mistakes and we ignore the potential for unscrupulous individuals to manipulate the system.

Having said that however due to the workings of the system that preceded this every attempt has been made to make the system fair. The Judges do their very best to ensure that a very fine line is not crossed between presumption of guilt and a presumption of innocence. Thus at the moment the tests are fair as far as the textbook definition goes. The only problem at present is the public perception interpretation of the evidence. DNA or fingerprints in their eyes prove guilt. Much of what has been discussed here would be a surprise to much of the public and indeed many people who have served as jurors in a forensic trial. This must be remedied, either by having a professional jury system, expert assesors or by placing limits on the media so that they do not misrepresent the forensic evidence. The simplification of the facts by the media over the years has led to this sorry situation.

That said, the obvious cases where there is so much supporting evidence that it would be unconscionable to find a not guilty verdict may in fact benefit from such a public view, it stops loopholes being found in a generally reliable evidential form. It is ironically the borderline cases that suffer. A guilty verdict on DNA evidence or fingerprints alone should be the exception and not the rule. This may be hard to accept in a rape or murder case but the philosophy of justice is clear. Justice applies to all people or not at all. While we hold justice dear we cannot make a sweeping burden for all accused to overcome that is so impossibly high that only the lucky few may pass the test.

The statistics are an amazingly hard problem, the jury set great store in them. So therefore surely we must remove them? No, to do so would be to make DNA on a par with fingerprints, totally reliable as far as the jury is concerned. It is a hard choice, impossibly high odds or a godlike reliability? There is no answer but to make DNA so reliable that it does in fact live up to its reputation, and to be honest with the jury to make sure they are indeed aware of the limitations of the evidence they are evaluating.

The experts should be constantly under scrutiny, their tests provide the basis for removing years of a man's life and thus the price must be worth paying even for one man. It would also add to the credibility of the evidence rather than detract from it. The past history of a well respected expert would work for him, and the track record of a new expert would mean that people would check the results. Granted this may lead to a new prosecutor's fallacy that a well respected expert is unchallengeable but this cannot be avoided if we start challenging their findings.

In short we can solve these problems by checking, checking and checking again. Only through brave individuals challenging the medium can our reliance on it ever be truly representative of its value. In America and in Britain lawyers have started to challenge the presumption, but for this to yield fruits the entire profession must start doing it. Only then can the system be changed to represent justice rather been seen to occasionally depart from it.

Once again it must be reiterated that only in a few cases does a miscarriage of justice occur in relation to DNA or fingerprint evidence but it is these cases that need to be examined for in them is the weakness of the entire criminal justice system. The price is simply not worth paying, for the reliance may spread and thus so will the injustice.

www.ingramcontent.com/pod-product-compliance
Lightning Source LLC
Chambersburg PA
CBHW071824170526
45167CB00003B/1410